The CAT IN THE HAT Knows a Lot About Christmas!

Written by Tish Rabe
Based on a television script by Karen Moonah
Illustrated by Joe Mathieu

A GOLDEN BOOK • NEW YORK

Visit us on the Web!
randomhouse.com/kids   Seussville.com   pbskids.org/catinthehat   treehousetv.com
Educators and librarians, for a variety of teaching tools, visit us at RHTeachersLibrarians.com
ISBN: 978-0-449-81495-6
Library of Congress Control Number: 2012954734
Printed in the United States of America
10 9 8 7 6 5 4 3 2 1
First Edition
Random House Children's Books supports the First Amendment and celebrates the right to read.

'Twas the day before Christmas and the Cat was excited.
He was having a party. All his friends were invited.
"Merry Christmas!" the Cat said. "I'm happy you're here.
Christmas is my favorite time of the year."
Pheasants brought presents, while starfish and bears
played find-the-candy-canes and musical chairs.
There was lots of good food—cookies, cakes, grubs, and slugs.
"Thank you, Cat," said a frog, "for this nice bowl of bugs."
"I'm so glad I came," said Fifi the Mouse.
"But I think I ate most of your gingerbread house!"

With the Cat's Christmas party under way in full swing,
a chorus of penguins decided to sing.
"Merry Christmas! Merry Christmas! Merry Christmas to you!
To the Cat in the Hat and to all his friends, too.
The food, the ornaments, the presents, the tree—
the Cat's Christmas party is the *place* to be."

The Fish wrote his list and was checking it twice.
"Some fin lotion," he said, "would be awfully nice.
I'd like a small bottle of Secrets of the Sea,
and Fin-tastic fish food would be dandy for me."

When the party was over, it was late Christmas Eve.

Little Ralph the Reindeer was ready to leave.

"Can you give me a ride, please? I cannot be late.

My parents are waiting so we can celebrate.

I live far away in cold Freeze-Your-Knees,

where there's lots of snow and we grow Christmas trees."

"Of course!" the Cat said. "Nick and Sally, let's fly!
Merry Christmas to all, and to all a goodbye!"
With a wave of his hand, they all flew out of sight,
but soon the Cat said, "Something doesn't feel right."

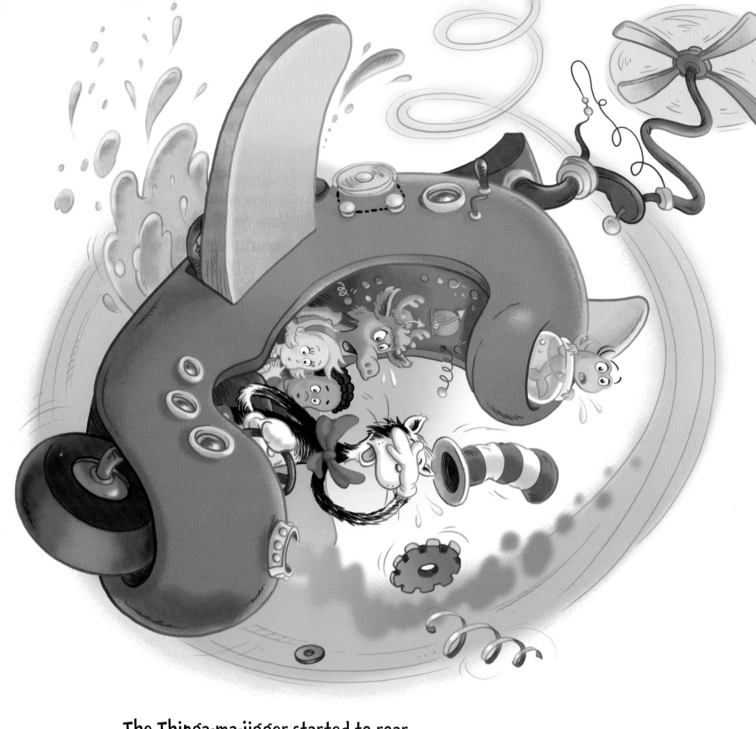

The Thinga-ma-jigger started to roar.

"What's that noise?" asked Nick. "Have you heard THAT before?"

"Oh no!" said the Cat. "The Toozle-tocker is ticking!

The Radia-toozle is leaking! The Stoppermatoggle is sticking!

We have to land. I can't see and can't steer.

Wherever we are—we are landing right here!"

They landed with a *bump-thump* on a dry, dusty plain.
"Where are we?" asked Ralph. The Cat tried to explain,
"In the Dusty-Vusty Veldt. It's all grassy and dry."
"But I live where it's snowy!" Ralph started to cry.

Then they heard a voice call, "Why, Cat, is that you?"
And a family of elephants came into view.
For the Cat has friends everywhere that he goes.
Wherever he is, there is someone he knows.
"Thimba!" the Cat said. "We need your help fast.
We've run out of water and that's why we crashed."
"We'll take you!" said Thimba. "Our trunks smell so well,
if there's water nearby, we'll be able to tell."

They jumped up on the elephants. While walking along,

the elephants sang their own Christmas song:

"At Christmas time we walk, you see,

together as a family.

We can smell water from far away.

We'll lead you to some water today!"

"Hurray!" Sally said. "I see water ahead!"
"Let's fill up so we can get going!" Nick said.

"Thank you," said the Cat. "The water did the trick."
"Now let's get Ralph home to his parents!" said Nick.

They quickly took off. Things went right for a while.
"I'll be home for Christmas!" Ralph said with a smile.
Then the Thinga-ma-jigger started to shake
and splutter and flutter and quiver and quake.
"Press the Floater-ma-boater! Immediately!
Or we'll crash with a splash into the deep sea!"

They dropped from the sky with a lolloping motion
and, sure enough, landed right smack in the ocean!
They crashed in the water with a very big splash.
Then three helpful dolphins showed up in a flash.

"We'll help you," one said, and he started to swim.

Then he burst into song and the others joined in.

"We *play* together! We *stay* together!

We're happy to pull you in.

We swim, we swish, but we're not fish.

We're happy to lend you a fin!"

The dolphins pushed the Thinga-ma-jigger onto the shore,
but it was still broken, the same as before.
"We're stranded," said Nick. "Now what do we do?"
"This is a job," said the Cat, "for Thing One and Thing Two!"

In minutes those Things stopped the Toozle-tocker from ticking,
the Radia-toozle from leaking, and the Stoppermatoggle from sticking!
"Great job!" said the Cat. "Oh, I'm so proud of you.
The Thinga-ma-jigger now looks good as new."

The Cat flipped the Jiggermawhizzer, but before they could fly
an army of red crabs came marching on by.
"Coming through! Look out! Take care!
We have to march from here to there.
Marching is what we like to do.
Merry Crabby Christmas to you!"

"Cat!" said Mervin the Crab. "My friend, how are you?
We're going to our Christmas party, and you can come, too."
"We would love to," the Cat said, "but I'm afraid we can't stay.
Ralph must get home to his folks right away."

The crabs waved their claws and called out, "Goodbye!
If you chance to see Santa Claus, please tell him hi!"

The Cat started the engine, but then something popped.

They went a few feet. Then they suddenly stopped.

"What's wrong?" asked Ralph. The Cat said, "I don't know.

It was working so well just a minute ago."

Now, there's a reason we all love the Cat as we do.

He thinks problems through and he finds answers, too!

"We can fix it!" he said. "I think I know how.
Nick and Sally, just open your Christmas gift now!"

The kids tore through the wrapping and, to their surprise,
found a Thinga-ma-jigger—exactly their size!
"Start 'er up!" said the Cat. "And take a quick ride
into the big one to check it inside."

Sally started to drive with a zag and a zig
and flew under the hood with a jag and a jig.
Once inside, Nick said, "Believe it or not,
it's even more awesome in here than I thought!"
"What's that noise?" Sally asked. And she called to the Cat,
"Something is banging! Cat, can you hear that?"
"It's inside the Dinner-ma-spinner," he said.
"Fly to the right and then go straight ahead."

"Sally!" a voice cried. "Help! I made a mistake!
I only came in for a bite of fruitcake.
I got in all right, but then, just my luck,
I tried to get out but I got really stuck."
"It's Fifi!" said Sally. "How can we get her out?"
"Look around," said the Cat, "for the Splutter-ma-spout.
Blow into it hard. And without any doubt,
poor little Fifi soon will pop out."

Nick took a big breath and he blew and he blew.
Fifi popped out and some crumbs popped out, too!

"To escape," said Fifi, "I just started chewing
through toggles and boggles—who knows *what* I was doing!"
"That's it!" said Nick. "So now we know why!
Without toggles and boggles, no WAY could we fly."
"I'm sorry," said Fifi, "and I've a long way to go.
Can I get home for Christmas? I don't really know."

"Fifi," said Sally, "what you need to do
is fly home in our new toy. It's perfect for you."
"Oh, thank you!" said Fifi. "I'll get home tonight!"
And with a twirl and a swirl, she flew out of sight.

"Push the Faster-ma-blaster!" the Cat said. "Let's go!
Let's get Ralph back to his home in the snow!"

Then off they flew through the Christmas Eve night
until Freeze-Your-Knees Snowland came into sight.
"Son!" said Ralph's mom. "We are so glad to see you."
"Mom! Dad!" said Ralph. "It's good to see you, too!"
"I tried," said the Cat, "to get him home on the double,
but the Thinga-ma-jigger had some engine trouble."
"That's okay," said Ralph's dad. "But we must leave right away.
Tonight we are going to pull Santa's sleigh."
"You're lucky!" said Nick. "What a fun thing to do.
I wondered who did that. Now I know it's *you*."

Dear SANTA,
My wish list...
- Secrets of the
  sea fin lotion
- Fin-tastic
  fish food
- A pink plastic
  castle
- A green deep-
  sea diver
Yours truly,
FISH
P.S. I've been
really good!

"I wrote a list," said the Fish, "but things got in the way.
Is it too late to send? It's almost Christmas Day."
"Give it to me," said Ralph. "I will take it myself
and give it to Santa, or maybe an elf."

"Let's go home, Cat," said Nick. "But before we do
Sally and I have a present for you."
"An ornament!" the Cat said. "It looks just like me!
I will hang this with pride on my Christmas tree.

"Christmas, my friends, is when reindeer go
back to their homes where they live in the snow.
Elephants walk to find water to drink,
and dolphins make sure that their friends do not sink.
Crabs march in line, their favorite thing,
and when they are marching, every crab likes to sing.

"And now as we fly through the sky, cold and clear,
I'm counting the days till it's Christmas . . . next year!"

Christmas Kitten,
Home at Last

Robin Pulver

paintings by Layne Johnson

ALBERT WHITMAN & COMPANY

Chicago, Illinois

For Bridget, Quinn, Riley, and Rachel, with love. —R.P.

Dedicated to the special kitties who have found a home in my heart, and warm thanks to my friends Karen Rudinger, Tim Scholten, and Courtney Sabotta. Ho, ho, ho! —L.J.

Library of Congress Cataloging-in-Publication Data
Pulver, Robin.
Christmas kitten, home at last / Robin Pulver ; paintings by Layne Johnson.
p. cm.
Summary: When Santa's allergies prevent him from keeping a homeless kitten,
he and Mrs. Claus find it a perfect home.
ISBN 978-0-8075-1157-2
[1. Cats—Fiction. 2. Santa Claus—Fiction. 3. Christmas—Fiction.]
I. Johnson, Layne, ill. II. Title.
PZ7.P97325Ck 2010
[E]—dc22
2009048123

The art was painted in oils on gessoed Arches paper.

The design is by Lindaanne Donohoe.

For more information about Albert Whitman & Company,
please visit our web site at www.albertwhitman.com.

The stars still shone bright when Santa arrived home from his most important journey of the year.

"This kitten is adorable," said Mrs. Claus. "Still, we mustn't get attached. Climb into bed for your nap, and I'll bring you a cup of hot cocoa. I bet we can find the perfect child and the perfect home for Cookie."

"It's too late for that," said Santa. "I've already made all my deliveries, and the elves are having their holiday party. Besides, we don't give pets for Christmas unless parents say it's OK."

"Santa," Mrs. Claus said, "we've been through this before. You don't have a cold. You're allergic to cats! You're allergic to Cookie!"

"That's true," said Santa, "b-but ... *Achooo!*"

Cookie leapt from Santa's arms to Mrs. Claus's.

"What's that?" asked Mrs. Claus. Santa blushed. "I found this kitten," he said. "He needs a home. I named him Cookie. Can we keep him?"

Mrs. Claus welcomed Santa home.

"How'd it go?" she asked.

"Perfect!" said Santa. "The reindeer were in top form. Smooth ride. No sticky chimney issues. Except—Achoo! I'm coming down with a cold."

"Rrrrr-rrrrr-rrrrrr...."

"You poor dear!" said Mrs. Claus. "It sounds like your cold has gone into your chest. I hear a rumbling in there."

"Meee-ow!"

He tucked his traveling companion inside his coat.
"Stay hidden, Cookie," he said. "I have some persuading
to do."

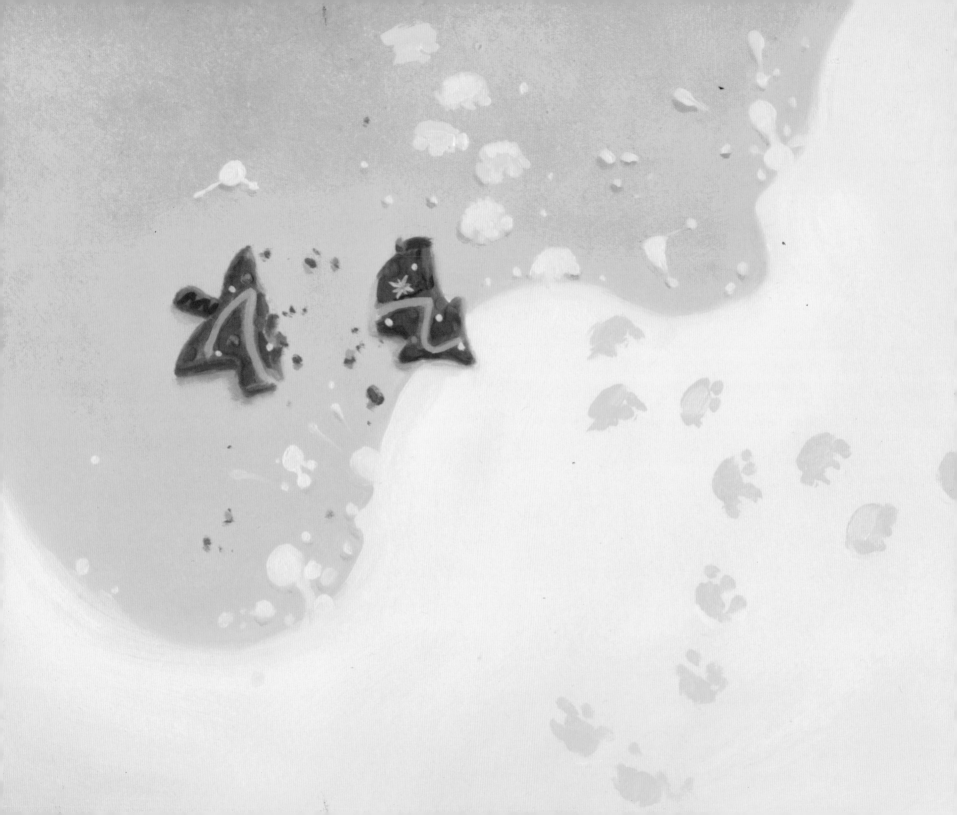

Santa carried the purring kitten to Angela's room. Cookie nestled snug against her.

Santa stifled a sneeze, so as not to wake the sleeping child. "The perfect home at last," he whispered. "Merry Christmas!"

Mrs. Claus insisted on driving, since Santa
hadn't had much of a nap.
"On, Comet! On, Blitzen!"
Away they all flew, to Angela's house.

"Thank you, elves!" shouted Santa. Then he whistled. "Blitzen! Comet! Just you two for an extra-quick trip. It's a light load!"

Santa's eyes twinkled. "This is the best part of my job: making a child's wish come true!"

Mrs. Claus tied a velvet ribbon around the kitten's neck and kissed his nose. "We'll miss you, Cookie," she said.

"My dear," Santa called, "why don't you come, too?"

"Santa, remember the letter from Angela?" said Mrs. Claus. "I think that our Cookie problem is solved."

"Achoo! I think so, too!" said Santa. "I can bear to part with him if he's going to the perfect home. Cookie, thank goodness you found this letter! I believe you know where you belong."

Two elves rushed up with a jingly, catnip-fragrant sack of brand-new kitten toys. They stowed it in Santa's sleigh.

Santa went back to sleep, but not for long.

CR-R-RASH!

Splash! SMASH!

THUD!

clatter-clatter-clank!

Santa sprang from his bed. He met Mrs. Claus in the kitchen.

On the floor lay pieces of a broken cookie jar and cookies.

"Never mind," said Mrs. Claus. "Kittens will be kittens. But…oh, look!…the eggnog!"

Mrs. Claus sighed. "Angela would be the perfect child for Cookie, if only…" She closed her eyes to think. She didn't notice when Cookie jumped down and scooted into the bedroom.

Cookie pounced on Santa's belly.

"Ho, ho! Oh, no! Achooo!"

Cookie tangled Santa's beard.

Achoo!

Achoo!

Achooo!

ACHOOOOOO!

"Meee-ow!" Cookie skedaddled.

Dear Santa,   December 5
My turtle died. Arnold was
a great turtle, and he lived a
long time.

Now I am lonely for a pet.
I would really like a kitten. But
cats are not allowed in our
apartment building. So what I'd
like for Christmas is a new rule
and a big sign that says:

KITTENS WELCOME!
♡
Angela ♡

Mrs. Claus found letters from children pleading for a kitten. They all promised to take good care of a pet. But none of the letters came with permission from parents.

The letter from Angela was especially touching:

Santa sighed and pulled the covers up. He fell fast asleep, worn out by his long journey.

"Come along, Cookie," said Mrs. Claus. "Let's peek in on the elves. Then we'll have another look through the mail."

As soon as Mrs. Claus had settled into her reading chair, Cookie curled up in her lap.

"Oh, dear," said Mrs. Claus. "I can see why Santa loves you so. But you can't stay here. Santa is frightfully allergic."

— The Givens —

December 19

Dear Santa,

We know it's late, but we have a special request. Our daughter, Angela, is sad. First, her pet turtle died. Then came our unexpected move to this new town. Angela had to say good-bye to her friends. Now she's afraid you don't know our new address.

We have our own house now, and a kitten would make it feel like a real home. Could you possibly bring Angela a kitten for Christmas? Our whole family would love and care for it.

Gratefully,

Carol and Chris Given

P.S. You'll know our house when you see it!

Beneath Santa's desk crouched the kitten, batting at an envelope.

"Unopened mail!" Santa exclaimed. "It must have fallen out of sight." He found his glasses and took out the letter. "This is not from a child," he said.

Santa and Mrs. Claus followed drippy pawprints all the way to the study.